G000080079

To:

....

On the Occasion of:

....

Date:

....

From:

....

Prayers
for
Living

Wendy Bray

A collection of prayers to help you invite a loving God
to share every twist and turn of your life's journey

Copyright © CWR, 2009

Published 2009 by CWR, Waverley Abbey House, Waverley Lane, Farnham, Surrey GU9 8EP, UK. Registered Charity No. 294387. Registered Limited Company No. 1990308.

The right of Wendy Bray to be identified as the author of this work has been asserted by her in accordance with the Copyright, Designs and Patents Act 1988, sections 77 and 78.

The Collects from *Common Worship: Services and Prayers for the Church of England* on pages 27 and 39 are copyright © The Archbishops' Council 2000 and are reproduced by permission.

For list of National Distributors visit www.cwr.org.uk/distributors

Unless otherwise indicated, all Scripture references are from the Holy Bible: New International Version (NIV), copyright © 1973, 1978, 1984 by the International Bible Society.

Other versions are marked:

GNB: Good News Bible, copyright © American Bible Society 1966, 1971, 1976, 1992, 1994.

The Message: Scripture taken from *The Message*. Copyright © 1993, 1994, 1995, 1996, 2000, 2001, 2002. Used by permission of NavPress Publishing Group.

NLT: Scripture quotations marked NLT are taken from the *Holy Bible*, New Living Translation, copyright © 1996, 2004. Used by permission of Tyndale House Publishers, Inc., Wheaton, Illinois 60189. All rights reserved.

Concept development, editing, design and production by CWR

Printed in China by C&C Offset Printers

ISBN: 978-1-85345-496-7

Contents

Introduction

Prayer is the lifeblood, lifeline and life-language of faith. We often forget the privilege we have in drawing closer to God in prayer. Prayer which frames a cry for help, guidance or wisdom. Prayer which includes spontaneous bursts of thanks and praise; our long wandering monologues of moaning and our sharp and painful 'Whys?' shot like a dart from a life of questions. God not only welcomes our prayers – from the whispered and the wordless to the yelled and carefully crafted – He *invites* them. Daily, minute by minute, in whatever circumstances we find ourselves, the God of the universe wants us to share our lives with Him in prayer: a holy conversation between Father and child, Creator and created. The privilege and possibilities of such an invitation – when accepted – are truly awesome.

The prayers in this book are not a comprehensive or adequate supply; they will not address every detail of our lives, neither will they meet all needs or scratch all itches! However, they will provide a starting point: somewhere to begin on those days when we don't know how to pray. They are written by ordinary people enjoying – and struggling with – ordinary faith. But they address a truly extraordinary God.

So, 'Let us pray' …!

All prayers are written by Wendy Bray,
unless otherwise stated.

01

FINDING THE *GOD* OF LIFE

'How do I find God?' It's the big question that has echoed through the lives of humans as long as they have been able to voice it.

For some of us, the search for God is a lifelong quest. We find Him, we begin to know Him, sometimes we fall out and then come back to Him, but we never quite know Him as much as we long to: He remains a mystery. Our relationship with God will always include that element of 'mystery' – that's the nature of faith. He invites us into the loving intimacy that can be found between Creator and created, between Father and child – but He is God, and we must still approach Him with awe.

These prayers begin at the beginning – with the search for God. They move on to include words of worship and thanksgiving as we begin to recognise our need for dependency on prayer in every area of our lives. These are prayers that could begin to cement our relationship with a God who searched for us long before we found Him.

Are you there, God?

God ...

I don't even know how to approach You;
How to address You;
Which words to use.

But lately I have been more aware of You.
I have sensed Your company at odd moments;
Felt Your gentle presence with me even
When I haven't asked for it.

It is as if You are waiting to introduce Yourself to me
With 'Don't I know you?'
Standing patiently in the margins of my life,
Longing to be more than just an onlooker.

So let me do the honours, God – because I am honoured.
Let me introduce myself to You.
Ah! I forgot – You already know me.
I just have to get to know You.
So here I am, God.
And here You are.

What next?

Desiring God

O Lord our God, grant us grace to desire you with a whole heart, so that desiring you we may seek you with a whole heart, so that desiring you we may seek and find you; and so finding you, we may love you; and loving you, may hate those sins which separate us from you, for the sake of Jesus Christ.

St Anselm of Canterbury (1033–1109)

Prayer before a step of faith

Here I stand, Lord God, about to take a step of faith.
Some call it a leap: a leap across a divide
from unbelief to belonging.
But I have edged slowly towards this place, beckoned
by You: attracted by Your story; Intrigued by
Your character; overwhelmed by Your love.
As I brace myself to jump – You hold out Your arms.
You'll catch me, hold me and lead me.
We're in this together.
And so the journey of faith begins …

Healing poem

My heart is like an iceberg:
not cold and hard
but seven-tenths hidden.
If I love you only
with the tenths that show,
my love won't last the course,
but if I am to love you with my whole heart,
I must face the pain
of hidden things
surfacing.
Come, Lord,
with the Titanic of your love.
Collide with my heart,
and in the great collision
Let it be my reservations
that sink forever.

GERARD KELLY, *SPOKEN WORSHIP*
(GRAND RAPIDS: ZONDERVAN, 2007) P.70.
USED BY PERMISSION.

PRAYERS OF WORSHIP AND THANKSGIVING

Sometimes – often for no particular reason – we feel a desire to praise and worship God and to thank Him for what He has done. A longing to worship is built into the fibre of those who choose the way of faith. Sometimes it's hidden by the stresses and strains of the day, quenched by disobedience or a sense of feeling far from God. But, we only have to begin to praise God with a spirit of thankfulness to know the kind of experience of worship that has joined – and continues to join – God's people across the world from the beginning of time and universally. A place of worship is a good place from which to begin to pray.

Shepherds praise

'Glory to God in the highest,
 and on earth peace to men on whom
his favour rests.'

<small>LUKE 2:14</small>

Praise for the God of Creation – from man's lowly position

O LORD, our Lord,
 how majestic is your name in all the earth!

You have set your glory
 above the heavens.
From the lips of children and infants
 you have ordained praise
because of your enemies,
 to silence the foe and the avenger.

When I consider your heavens,
 the work of your fingers,
the moon and the stars,
 which you have set in place,
what is man that you are mindful of him,
the son of man that you care for him?

PSALM 8:1–4

King David's prayer of praise

Praise be to you, O Lord,
 God of our father Israel,
 from everlasting to everlasting.
Yours, O Lord, is the greatness and the power
 and the glory and the majesty and the splendour,
 for everything in heaven and earth is yours.
Yours, O Lord, is the kingdom;
 you are exalted as head over all.
Wealth and honour come from you;
 you are the ruler of all things.
In your hands are strength and power
 to exalt and give strength to all.
Now, our God, we give you thanks,
 and praise your glorious name.

1 Chronicles 29:10–13

A thankyou prayer

Sometimes …
Thankyou should be a bigger word.
A fatter word; a louder word.
It should burst at the seams and clang like noisy cymbals.
Be shouted from the rooftops or held
high on a blazing banner.

Sometimes …
Thankyou should be a softer word.
A whispered word; heartfelt relief in every breath.
It should fall with honest intimacy at Your feet.
Be nestled gently against the comfort You give.

So … whether sung in a song, muttered in a muddled
moment or lifted heavenward in simple silence:

THANKYOU, Father!

Faith means that worship and thanksgiving are part of our lives whatever happens to us. There will be times when we must choose to praise God – for He is still God. The prayers that follow are prayers that reflect a 'whatever' faith: the kind of faith shown by Daniel (Daniel 3:18) and, eventually, Habakkuk.

Habakkuk's 'prayer'

Though the fig-tree does not bud
 and there are no grapes on the vines,
though the olive crop fails
 and the fields produce no food,
though there are no sheep in the pen
 and no cattle in the stalls,
yet I will rejoice in the LORD,
 I will be joyful in God my Saviour.

HABAKKUK 3:17–18

The 'Yet Prayer' – after Daniel and Habakkuk

Lord, I pray that You will take away this suffering;
ease my burden, still my unquiet heart.
Yet even if You do not, I will praise You,
Lord God, Suffering Servant.

Lord, I pray that You will intervene in this situation;
by Your power make changes for the better.
Yet even if You do not, I will thank You,
Lord God, Powerful One.

Lord, I pray that You will give escape
from all that fills me with fear;
offer a way out rather than a way through.
Yet even if You do not, I will praise You,
Lord God, Eternal Refuge.

Lord, I pray that You will save me from what lies ahead;
throw a lifeline, lift me out.
Yet even if You do not, I will praise You,
Lord God, Merciful Saviour.

Lord, I pray that You will lead me beside quiet waters,
that the valley of the shadow will not include my pathway.
Yet even if You do not, I will praise You,
Lord God, Faithful Shepherd.

Yet I will rejoice; yet I will rejoice!
Yet I will rejoice in the Lord!
I will be joyful in God, my Saviour.
For He is my God.

And finally, a little prayer for humility
never goes amiss ...

The ant prayer

Here I sit, Lord God
And here You are next to me.
Creator of the earth;
Mighty King;
Lord of All.
The Architect of the universe;
The Artist whose brush has swept the sky
into place and scattered it with stars;
The Great Big God.

I feel so small, Lord;
So very tiny.
Like a speck on a white page.
Humbled.
A micro-me.

Now I know why You created ants.

❧ 02 ❧

PRAYING
THROUGH
THE
SEASONS
OF LIFE

*Life is lived through seasons. Not just seasons of the
calendar but seasons of humanity. We are born, we grow,
we learn, we do our best day to day. Our dreams are
fulfilled or we are left disappointed. These prayers are
prayers of the 'everyday' and the familiar: of work and
play, of celebration and circumstance. They are words
with which we might surround both the mundane and
the marvellous detail of life. But most of all, they are
about change.*

*In times of uncertainty we need to know that our God
is unchanging; that He is the same from generation to
generation, the same whatever befalls us: loving and
dependable, always to be trusted. He never forgets us –
our lives are written on the palms of His hands (Isaiah
49:16). He is the God of our past and our present: the God
of eternity. We may not know what the future holds but
we know who holds the future.*

A Morning Collect

Almighty and everlasting God,
we thank you that you have brought us safely
to the beginning of this day.
Keep us from falling into sin
or running into danger,
order us in all our doings
and guide us to do always
what is righteous in your sight;
through Jesus Christ our Lord.
Amen.

Prayer for today

Lord,
This day will be dictated by the clock;
peopled by both those I love and those I don't know;
soundtracked by noise, traffic, chattering and laughter.
This day will go faster than I can keep up with.
By turn it will be harder than I thought
and easier than I hoped;
promise more and deliver less than I anticipated.
This day will be just like yesterday – but entirely different.
A prelude to tomorrow – but full of its own time.
It will never come again – and will soon be far behind.
But most of all this day is Your gift.
Don't let me waste a minute of it!

School – a prayer to pray with children

Father God, we'd like to talk to You about school.
Sometimes we love it – and sometimes
we don't want to go at all.
But that's OK with You.
We know that You always walk there with us.
You run into the playground with our friends.
You sit with us as we listen and watch over us as we work.
You encourage us when we get stuck, and
celebrate with us when we do well.
You know all the secret things that make
us feel sad or worried – we can share them
with You exactly when they happen.

So as we go to school today:
Keep us safe on the journey to and fro.
Give our teachers wisdom and strength
– and laughter in their hearts.
Help us to be happy with our friends
and kind to those who aren't.
Inspire us to listen and learn and enjoy new things.
Be with our family and friends
whatever they are doing today.
And give us all space and time to share our day
at the end of it with You and with each other.

Prayer in the search for work – after Moses (Exodus 3)

In the search for work, our hearts will often long to hook into God's wider purposes for the world, whatever our role or task. God delights in that longing and makes the place where we are standing holy ground just by being there – but He also calls us from that place to work for Him.

I don't get Moses, Lord God.
He wasn't even looking for work, but You called him.
He made every excuse in the book, but You equipped him.
He didn't know where he was going, but You sent him.
Call me – I'll go.
Equip me – I'm ready.
Send me – I'll go where You go ahead of me.
Fill my heart with Your passion;
Help me share Your purpose;
Have a part in Your plan.

Whatever shape work is.
Stand me on holy ground – then I'll begin.

Prayer before a difficult week at work

Father, this week will be really hard for me.
Please so infuse me with Your Spirit that Your love
fills my entire mind, not leaving any empty corners.

Father, give me the grace to bear with
those people I find difficult.
Where I feel bad, anxious, nervous, or even hateful,
please remove those feelings by Your Spirit.
Give me the mercy to forgive – help me to
remember the words of Your Son:
'Forgive us our sins as we forgive
those who sin against us.'

Father, help me to remember why I need to
get out of bed every morning this week:
I need to serve You! I need to direct other
people to You! I need to worship You with
my whole being, just being who I am!

So Father, with Your help, this week
doesn't have to be hard.
May I remember this prayer.
May I remember what Your Word says: I can be holy
in all my conduct because He who calls me is holy!

Go with me into this week Lord!

Martyn Ingham

Moving house

Lord God,
We've packed up our belongings, now
we must pack up our memories.
They are as mixed as the contents
of these boxes at our feet.
They fill the empty rooms we are about to leave,
reminding us of celebrations, homecomings, days of
bad news, arguments and laughter in mixed measure.
These walls are marked by the knocks of our
life; painted the colour of our dreams.
But they will soon surround the dreams of others.
We must move on to build future
memories in a new home.
But You are already there, ahead of us, and as we
shut this door, You will be on the other
side of a new one. Forever.

Prayer of an empty nester

This silence, Lord!
No loud music, no aimless chatter, no
laughter ringing down the stairs.
Even the tidiness is getting to me. There are no
discarded shoes to trip over; no small crowds
of mugs and empty plates in every corner.
Today I am trying hard not to wander
into their bedrooms lest I cry.
Trying not to stop before their baby
photographs and look back over the years.
Where did those days go?

Father, I know You gave them to me
to raise for this very time.
I know that they must make their way in the world
without me: leave home; study and work away from my
watchful eye: and that they are always under Yours.
But letting go is so much harder
than I imagined it would be!
Thank You that You understand what it is
to watch a son leave home; You feel the pain
of a far-off daughter; You know the physical
wrench of separation from those You love.
Help me to find ways to love them at a distance
(without embarrassment on their part!) and
keep them safe in Your love, Father.
Prompt them to phone occasionally; help me share their
new world and their enthusiasm in it and remind me that
there are others here at home who still need my care.
… And when I *do* give in to the tears, comfort
me with anticipation of the laughter to come: of
the celebration of homecoming – and the joy of
discarded shoes, loud music and aimless chatter.
Oh how I love it, Lord!

Prayer for one not retired but just re-treaded

How did I get here, Lord?
Seems like just last week that I took that first job.
Before I noticed, it was the handshake, the card, the party.
All those jokes about greenhouses and grandchildren ...
then I realised they were for me!

Lord – I don't feel old enough to retire.
Yet some days I certainly feel ready.
I may even have longed for this day, if I'm honest.
So, what next, Lord?
The job may be over – but there's still work to be done.
This isn't the beginning of the end –
it's the end of the beginning.
Dare I hope that the best is yet to be?

Don't retire me Lord – just make sure I'm re-treaded.
Ready to hit a new road: and not
necessarily into the sunset!

So where to next, Lord?

Prayer for older age

Heavenly Father,
My days seem long – remind me that
each one is a gift from You.
The nights are longer – be by my
side when sleep evades me.
My weeks are often empty – fill them
with Your purposes still.

Have me know that it is in these twilight days that
I can do the most secret, the most hidden, the
most wonderful work of Your kingdom through
prayer – and just by loving those You send to me.

As my memory fades, my eyesight dims
and my feet are unsure of their path,
keep me ever mindful that I am not forgotten by You;
I am always in Your sight and that – one day – You
will lead me home to be welcomed by the words:

'Well done, good and faithful servant.'

An Evening Collect

Lighten our darkness,
Lord, we pray,
and in your great mercy
defend us from all perils and dangers of this night,
for the love of your only Son,
our Saviour Jesus Christ.
Amen.

03

PRAYERS INVITING GOD INTO THE *RELATIONSHIPS* THAT GIVE OUR LIVES MEANING

We live out our lives and our relationships in the sight of a Father God who loves and cares for us. Because we are His children, He also knows a little about the ups and downs of family life! But, of course, we also form and maintain relationships beyond our families, and God requires us to have a special place in our hearts for those who have no family (Psalm 68:6; James 1:27).

God is a God of relationship: He loves His interaction with us and He places a high priority on the integrity, love and self-sacrifice we show in our relationships with each other. These prayers help us to focus on making our relationships 'God-shaped'.

Prayer for a friend

Father, I thank You for this most
precious gift of friendship.
For the dry and the fertile days that have grown its love;
The rough places that have honed its patience;
The investment of trust that has developed its loyalty.
Thank You for the shared joy of laughter
and the shared burden of tears.
Bless my dear friend at this moment and be
her guide, her inspiration, her comfort.
Be all that she needs that I can never be.
And be there for her as she has always been for me.

Marriage: a prayer to pray together

Lord, the two of us have promises to keep.
Some days they will sit easy in our hearts.
Some weeks they will be strained and close to brokenness.
Be with us every hour.

Remind us that sometimes love will be an
act of will, not a choice of 'won't'.
That our words can wound as deeply as they can comfort.
Teach us love that is about meeting each
other's needs, not prioritising our own.
Give us grace in forgiveness; comfort
in sorrow; thanksgiving in joy.
May our marriage be both an act of
worship and a source of delight.
And help us keep you at its centre.

Mother's prayer for an unborn child

Lord, today I felt this little one move; like a
butterfly flickering in the depths of my being.
What an awesome responsibility You have given me! To
carry the life You have ordained from conception to birth.
I am flushed with wonder at the way You are doing
Your part: 'knitting together' as the psalmist says,
until this child is 'perfectly and wonderfully made'.
Give me patience in each day of waiting; peace about
all that lies ahead and the strength to do my part.
And thank You, Lord: for the privilege, for the
excitement, for the honour of motherhood.
Bless this baby – and may he one day know
You: as Saviour, Lord and giver of Life.

Happy birth-day

Lord, we rejoice in this happy birth-day.
Thank You for this child born to us,
just as You planned;
One given to us to love and care for
all the days of his life.
Grant us patience, energy,
strength and wisdom.

… And in these first days, Lord –
please give us sleep!

Fostering and adoption

Lord,
As we welcome this precious child
into our lives, how we rejoice!
Rejoice at a homecoming.
Rejoice at the gifts of parenthood and compassion.
Rejoice in Your protection and care for Your children.

As we face the days ahead, teach us to rely on You, Lord.
As the faithful Father of all.
As the Giver of wisdom and patience.
As the Source of all love.

And, Lord ... may we have fun!!

Children

'As for my family and me, we will serve the Lord.'
(Joshua 24:15 [GNB])

Thank you Lord for your promises. Help me to hold on tight to your word and to trust in your wonderful love for me, and for my children. I fear for them, for their future, and for the people they will love. But I will trust in you and I will remember your words of comfort: That my children are your children too. God of Love, I praise you.

Amen

Karine Law

Grandparents' prayer

Father,
It seems like only yesterday that we became parents
ourselves.
And now this day has come and our child is a parent too.
As we visit for the first time, remind us what
it is like to be in their shoes: the tiredness, the
anxiety, the ups and downs of emotion.
Inspire us with wisdom, with understanding, with
kindness and with humour. Show us how to allow
our children to be parents their way – not ours.
Help us know when to speak and when to stay
quiet; when to act and when to leave well alone!
In the years ahead, help us love them, care
for them, support and encourage them.
And as we look into the face of our new
grandchild, show us something of the wonder
of Your own amazing parenthood.

For a homecoming

Someone I love is coming home today, Father.
I can barely contain my excitement!
The long days of waiting are over and soon that
beloved, familiar face will be before me.
There's so much to do in preparation!
I want everything to be just as they remembered:
the food, our home, their special places.
Fill us with joy that we are bold in expressing;
love that recognises deepest needs and a
spirit of celebration and thankfulness.
And amidst it all, remind us that You know –
and anticipate – the joy of homecoming.

So many of our prayers about relationships surround a need for grace and forgiveness, acceptance and loving against the odds. These prayers dig a little deeper into those needs ...

Prayer for forgiveness in anger

Heavenly Father, You know what it is to be
angry; to forgive; to weep; to be betrayed; to be
isolated. There is not one tiny sensation of human
experience that You do not understand fully.
Therefore, we can bring our burden of anger before
You, even as we stagger under its weight. And we
can leave it with You, at the foot of the cross where
Your Son cried out to save us from ourselves.
Thank You, Father, for Your forgiveness, Your
love, Your grace, Your mercy and Your justice.
Hold us in Your arms, Lord.
Amen.

Wendy Bray and Chris Ledger, *Insight into Anger*
(Farnham: CWR, 2007) p.117.

After an argument

I wanted the last word, Lord.
But now my word – of apology – needs to be the first.
Whether I 'feel like it' or not.
Let me drop all thoughts of 'blame'
and 'fault' or 'who started it'.
Instead, let me be the one to 'start it' this time:
to start the process of reconciliation.
Let there be no 'ifs' and 'buts', no 'and another things'.
Let there be less of the dregs of resentment
and more first sips from the cup of peace.
I'm going there now, Lord: to that place
I want to be a place of forgiving.
Give me grace, patience – and huge amounts of love.

(And forgive us, Lord …)

Help me forgive

Lord God,
It is so hard to forgive.
The pain is too deep, the words
too many, the outrage too loud.
Help me just to begin to want to
forgive, believing that You will
do the rest.

Lord God

Help me love the unlovable;
forgive the unforgiveable;
hold the untouchable
And walk the impossible path …

Just because Your path led to
the cross, for me.

A prayer for a transformed heart

Lord Jesus, only you can transform my heart and
give me a spirit of genuineness and forgiveness.
I need your eyes to see beyond a person's harsh façade
and your love to accept a person just as they are.
Help me to see my own heart and lead me to repentance
and humility, that I may be open to you and others.
That I may connect with someone's deepest
hopes and fears, so they may know your love.
God of forgiveness, truly, I worship you.

KARINE LAW

Prayer for forbearance

Lord,
I need Your patience and forbearance today.
This visit will be difficult – make me brave!
The conversation will not be easy
– give me the right words.

I may feel angry, aggrieved, offended, misunderstood.
Help me listen with grace, with insight, with a
desire to understand the other's point of view,
however misguided, selfish or unreasonable.
Help me to speak less than I might and only as
much as I ought – with plain words of wisdom.

You know what it is to be wrongly
accused, insulted, labelled, abused.
You were the victim of miscarriage
of justice, of bribery, of lies.
Yet out of it all you brought reconciliation and love.

Help me today to see a way to do the same.

04

FACING
THE
STORMS
AND THE
DESERTS
OF LIFE

Our lives of faith are journeys, and like any journey we will often pass through terrain that is less than comfortable. However, these stormy, dark or dry places are as valuable a part of the faith journey as the lush green fields and easy, meandering paths. In fact, they are often more so: in the Bible it is in these difficult places that God often speaks most powerfully. But knowing that doesn't always help us get through. So, these prayers are to help us put one weary foot in front of the other, clinging on to what faith we have, however weak it seems. Some of these prayers are from the Psalms, that collection of often brutally honest prayers and songs that express so well the agonies and ecstasy of faith. They are sometimes raw with pain, laced with anger, often confused and perhaps even misguided. However, they are a reminder that the God we know not only hears our prayers – whatever we might feel – He also identifies with us. He is the loving Father, the suffering Son and the promised Comforter who does not leave us alone in our pain, our darkness or our desert place but joins us there.

When doubting

Just as I am, though tossed about
With many a conflict, many a doubt,
Fightings within, and fears without
O lamb of God, I come.

<small>CHARLOTTE ELLIOTT (1789–1871)</small>

When feeling forsaken

My God, my God, why have you forsaken me?
 Why are you so far from saving me,
 so far from the words of my groaning?
O my God, I cry out by day, but you do not answer,
 by night and am not silent.

Yet you are enthroned as the Holy One;
 you are the praise of Israel.
In you our fathers put their trust;
 they trusted and you delivered them.
They cried to you and were saved;
 in you they trusted and were not disappointed.

PSALM 22:1–5

Seeking God – when He seems far away

As the deer pants for streams of water,
 so my soul pants for you, O God.
My soul thirsts for God, for the living God.
 When can I go and meet with God?
My tears have been my food day and night,
while men say to me all day long,
 'Where is your God?'
These things I remember as I pour out my soul:
how I used to go with the multitude,
 leading the procession to the house of God,
with shouts of joy and thanksgiving
 among the festive throng.

Why are you downcast, O my soul?
Why so disturbed within me?
Put your hope in God,
 for I will yet praise him,
my Saviour and my God.

Psalm 42:1–6

Sometimes in our sense of isolation and doubt it is important to be honest with God, however raw that honesty. What God asks for is relationship with us. Just to 'keep talking' means that we continue to communicate with Him even if we doubt the value of that communication or see no sign of His presence in our lives.

Here are three poems written as prayers at a time when expressing pain in prayer was just too difficult.

God has left the building

*This prayer was written after a telephone conference call,
the form of which helped the writer express exactly how
she felt about the apparent absence of God.*

Today my God has left the building.
Taken His feet from beneath the
conference table that is my life;
Finished His presentation and closed His portfolio.
I am no longer on the agenda.
Not even tagged on as 'any other business'.
He has become the sleeping Partner.

Graffiti

If I could write graffiti on the walls that
curve around my path to heaven,
It would read 'No comfort'.
Even for those who love and trust in You.
'There is no comfort.'
Only the blackness of the night
And the emptiness of my heart.
'There is no comfort.'
Only my dreams of longing to be held.
'There is no comfort.'
Though I cry out against the wall, the
dark, the tears, even the dreams
Through the long watches of the night

'THERE IS NO COMFORT!'

Prayer to a Hidden God

I used to think there was a point in
even the greatest suffering:
A glimmer of hope; some small triumph;
A victory cry running through the veins of pain.
But there is none.
There is no point but the stabbing point that wounds.
There is only God.
Yet even He hides Himself in dark draperies.
He waits concealed behind walls of silence
or lurks in the shadows of hopelessness,
so that I cannot recognise Him.
Like Mary, with tears that blur her vision, I cry, 'Master?'
But I don't hear His voice.
Unlike her, I do not leap to my feet. I sink to the floor.
Lost.
There is no point;
Only a hidden God.

Prayer for the end of a dark day

Oh God! Today has been the worst of days.
A Good Friday kind of a day.
My eyes are sore from weeping;
my heart is breaking with disbelief;
my body aches just from breathing through each hour.
Praying is the last thing I want to do –
but the first thing I need to do.
For there is nowhere and no one to
go to, Lord, but to You.
I may rage at You, hurl insults that shame
me the moment they have left my lips, send
my blaming and wailing heavenward.
But you take it all, Lord.
Your shoulders are broad enough;
Your wisdom deep enough.
You count my tears, absorb my grief,
hear my harrowing cries.
For they echo Your cries from the cross:
'My God, my God, why have you forsaken me?'

Remind me, Lord, that under those dark skies You shared my suffering; You felt my pain; bore my shame; knew this desolation. Not just to save me but to identify with me, So that with tenderness You could say, as You do now, 'I know, I know …' and stay with me through this dark night.

As I sit here with You, spent and weak; bewildered and empty, help me to find something with which to trust that Easter Sunday does follow Good Friday. That joy does follow grief, and that even in this deep darkness, a tiny glimmer of the light of hope can be found; that the morning will come and that I can – and will – praise You once more.

Sometimes all we can do is wait for God ...

I am still confident of this:
I will see the goodness of the Lord
 in the land of the living.
Wait for the Lord;
 be strong and take heart
 and wait for the Lord.

PSALM 27:13–14

Psalm 23 – as a prayer acknowledging peace and trust

The LORD is my shepherd, I shall not be in want.
 He makes me lie down in green pastures,
he leads me beside quiet waters,
 he restores my soul
He guides me in paths of righteousness
 for his name's sake.
Even though I walk
 through the valley of the shadow of death,
I will fear no evil,
 for you are with me;
your rod and your staff,
 they comfort me.

You prepare a table before me
 in the presence of my enemies.
You anoint my head with oil;
 my cup overflows.
Surely goodness and love will follow me
 all the days of my life,
and I will dwell in the house of the LORD
 for ever.

❧ 05 ❧

Living
Daily
with the
Lord
of Life

*The journey of faith is travelled largely in the 'everyday'
– and never remains the same for long. One moment we
can find ourselves on spiritual mountain tops, enjoying
the view, in another moment we are alone and thirsty
in the desert. Each day of the journey requires our
dependence on a faithful God, who, whatever we feel,
promises never to leave us (Deuteronomy 31:6).*

*By its nature, a life of faith also involves living alongside
other Christians, being part of the church community,
struggling with sin, finding God's will, trying to live out
our faith in a world that largely rejects faith – but is often
intrigued – and just getting on with the tricky business of
living. These prayers aim to help us on our way.*

Prayer for every day

Lord,
You never said this life of faith would be easy.
But some days it's more than hard.
I don't 'feel' Your presence.
I can't even begin to pray.
I lose patience with my family
And don't want to be with my friends.
It's a struggle even to want to do Your will.
And I don't seem to care if I can't.

But You know all that.
And I know that while You don't expect
perfection, You do long for relationship;
That we won't see me change overnight
but I am a work in progress.
A work designed, wept over and blessed by its Creator.

More than anything, remind me of Your
Astounding love;
Inexplicable grace;
Infinite patience;
Never-ending faithfulness,
Towards this wayward, hopeful, tries-hard child of Yours.

The knitting prayer

Lord God,
You 'knit me together in my mother's womb'.
You cast me on all those years ago and
You're still knitting:
Row by row in the click-click of life.
You design the pattern, I follow.
You unravel the knots.
You stretch me a bit.
And together we shape a life that fits
Your purposes perfectly.
I wear it as I go; unfinished yet perfectly styled,
marvelling at its ability to grow with me.
Not a 'one size fits all', 'off the peg' knitted
life, but tailormade: Designer labelled,
with a lifetime guarantee.
I'll wear it with pride until it's time to cast off;
time to be fitted for a really heavenly garment.

But for now.
Click, click.
Keep me in your pattern Lord.

Church life – a lighthearted prayer for patience and grace

Lord, why is this church like a box of assorted
Christmas biscuits in January?

I remember how I slid off the glossy presentation
packaging with such excitement;
lifted the lid with anticipation and delight.
The neatly ordered contents stared up at me – each
member in its place, fresh and crisp and full of promise:
a luxury assortment, waiting for me to dive in.
But now they've been around a while
they're losing their appeal;
I've poked around underneath and I'm disappointed;
They're getting a bit stale, going a bit soft.
'Love me!' they said. So I loved them.
But they are never quite what they seem. They
crumble and crack, fall apart in the middle, get
chocolate chips on their shoulders and make
a mess of my nice neat Christian outfit.
They give me committee toothache and
worship style wind; their doctrinal peculiarities
stick to the roof of my mouth.

I can't stomach them much longer.
Morning coffee leaves me feeling lonely
and digestive the sermons are not.
And those layers of self-importance:
the top drawer and the bottom!
So many trying to be a spiritual jam cream
or a glossy, gold-foiled double chocolate.
Everyone ignoring the sweet, thin
Nice one and dear old Marie.
Anyway, I never find myself with the gold foils:
I always end up with the plain, boring ones that
nobody else wants; trying to make them feel
important by choosing them, reluctantly.

I've had enough of them all Lord – they make me sick!

But ...

maybe if I realised that I'm not above them
all – that it's not for me to pick and choose, I
might discover something surprising?
What if I gave equal attention to the
top layer and the bottom?
Didn't always go for the ones that stand out but gave the
less attractive ones a chance? If I accepted them all as
necessary to the assortment – each one its own variety?
Perhaps I should look at them for what they really
are? Fragile, broken and already chosen – by You.

Lord – teach me to be a better biscuit lover.

The following prayers help us to face up to our selfish ways of living, acknowledge our sin and turn back to God – something we all need to do regularly. David's prayer from the Psalms is a beautiful and eloquent prayer of confession: his words are so relevant, human and honest that we can make them our own. Martyn Ingham's prayers give the theme a contemporary touch while James Jones includes God's response to a repentant and truly sorry heart.

Prayer for forgiveness – a prayer of David

Have mercy on me, O God,
 according to your unfailing love;
according to your great compassion
 blot out my transgressions.
Wash away all my iniquity
 and cleanse me from my sin …

Surely you desire truth in the inner parts;
 you teach me wisdom in the inmost place.

Cleanse me with hyssop and I shall be clean;
 wash me, and I shall be whiter than snow …

Create in me a pure heart, O God,
 and renew a steadfast spirit within me.

PSALM 51:1–2,6–7,10

Acknowledging – and dealing with – sin

Lord, why do I sin?

Father, You know what I have done.
You know what I haven't done – what
I have neglected to do.
You see what I do in secret.
You see and hear the very thoughts of my heart.
I cannot escape Your knowledge of me.
Please help me to understand the
things which lead me to sin.
Please help me to dig up the pathways
which take me there.
Please hold my hand and lead me down pure roads.
Please bring light to my path – and my mind.
Please help me to remember Your Word.
I love You, Lord!

MARTYN INGHAM

Rubbish!

'There's something between me and The Father
Something that holds me back from Him;
I want to run and jump into His arms
Yet something lies between me and
Him: the rubbish of sin.'

Lord, give me the strength I need to
empty all the bins in my life.
Filled with all the rubbish I have accumulated.
I put in:
The peel from the fruits of this world;
The wrappings from little pleasures
I have momentarily enjoyed;
The used teabags from the cups from
which I should not have drunk;

The plastic bags in which I have
carried around my burdens;
The leftovers from the worldly feasts I have tucked into –
I am determined not to re-heat them,
but to throw them away;
The broken plates, smashed in my anger and frustration;
The dirt and dust I have walked into this
house – this temple of Your Spirit.
You have provided the black bags
– I just need to fill them.
I will leave them outside my life and my mind, and You
will come and collect them and take them away. For good.

Martyn Ingham

Prayer asking God for forgiveness

Lord,
I have kept silent too long.
I have presumed upon your kindness.
I have left undone those things I should have done
And have done those things I should not have done.
I have kicked over the traces
through my own deliberate fault.
I have spoken words of destruction.
I have painted pictures with my mind
That would shame my closest friend.
I have done that which is evil in your sight.
Peace and blessing have been strangers to me.

Instead of seeking your face, I have sought excuses.
Instead of confessing my transgression
I have sought to justify myself.
Instead of coveting your forgiveness
I have comforted myself with vanities:
'It's natural', 'I'm human', 'Everybody is like it.'
Lord, I confess my transgression.

Lord Jesus have mercy upon me.

My child
I forgive you
The guilt is gone
Go in peace
I forgive you.

JAMES JONES, *PEOPLE OF THE BLESSING* (ABINGDON: BRF, 1998)

PP.24–25. USED BY PERMISSION.

The Lord's prayer – for His disciples (two versions)

'Father,
hallowed be your name,
your kingdom come.
Give us each day our daily bread.
Forgive us our sins,
 for we also forgive everyone
 who sins against us.
And lead us not into temptation.'

LUKE 11:2–4

'Father,
Reveal who you are.
Set the world right.
Keep us alive with three square meals.
Keep us forgiven with you and
forgiving others.
Keep us safe from ourselves and the Devil.'

LUKE 11:2–4, THE MESSAGE

A prayer for life

'I will be your God throughout your lifetime – until your hair is white with age, I made you, and I will care for you. I will carry you along and save you.' (Isaiah 46:4 [NLT])

Lord, I thank you that my life is in your hand
and I am so grateful that you saved me.
Continue to guide and help me until the day I die.
My heart is touched deeply at the thought
of seeing you, and holding you.
Until then, flood me with your love and
let me be your light in the darkness.
For your Glory Jesus.
Amen.

KARINE LAW

PRAYERS THAT EXPRESS A LONGING TO HEAR GOD AND BE GUIDED BY HIM

All of us will, at some point in our lives, long to hear God speak into our situation in some way. We'll seek guidance when confused, assurance when bewildered and comfort when distressed. God does sometimes speak in a clearly audible voice but He also speaks through His Word, His creation, our circumstances and in the wise words of others. We only have to be willing to listen, to hear ... and to respond.

Samuel to God

'Speak, for your servant is listening.'

1 SAMUEL 3:10

Get in touch

If only You sent emails, Lord God – or texts.
Just one or two words to give me a clue.
Drop me a line, won't you? Get in touch.
It needn't be writing in the sky or letters
etched on tablets of stone.
I don't need poems of renown or prose of importance.
Just a word or two of direction,
encouragement, affirmation.
As I learn to listen, read and watch, teach me to
hear Your voice in the utterances of others, in the
pages of Your Word, in the beauty of Your world.
Help me to listen not just with my ears but with my heart.
Not just for what I usually hear but
for what I don't expect.
Give me discernment, wisdom, insight, knowledge.
And when I *do* hear You, read You, see You,
loud and clear, prompt me to act, to speak.
To love and to live in the very echoes of Your voice.

And some words of blessing ...

A blessing

'The LORD bless you
 and keep you;
the LORD make his face shine upon you
 and be gracious to you;
the LORD turn his face towards you
 and give you peace.'

NUMBERS 6:24–26

The blessing

May you who are restless
find rest,
and in rest, restoration
and the healing
of your hollow soul.
May peace be yours.

May you who are frozen
find freedom,
and in freedom, the strength
to face the fire
and the thawing
of your ice-gripped heart.
May peace be yours.

May you who are conflicted
find convergence,
and in convergence, confidence
to be the one new child
of your old divided self.
May peace be yours.

May you who live in tension
find tenderness,
and in tenderness, the tendency
to kindness
and the miracle
of majoring in mercy.
May peace be yours.

And you who are God-less,
may you find God,
and in God,
the grace and growth you need
for fruit and fullness
and the love that will last you
through the long haul
of a lived-for-others life.
May peace be yours.

GERARD KELLY, *SPOKEN WORSHIP*
(GRAND RAPIDS: ZONDERVAN, 2007) PP.20–21.
USED BY PERMISSION.

06

Prayers that Frame a Life Lived *Abundantly*

One of the most exciting things about a life lived with God is the way in which we are part of His Big Story. Our names are written into His plans for the world; we are cast members in the most exciting adventure story ever.

These final prayers celebrate our life in God: both the everyday shared celebrations and the personal joys. They also focus our attention on God's purpose for us and help us look forward to an eternity with Him. There are prayers that dream; prayers of thanksgiving; prayers of hope. We also come back to where we began: prayers of worship. Each one celebrates a community life and an individual life lived to the full – and into eternity in the knowledge and love of God.

The dream prayer

Father God
Set a dream in my heart
Help me to trace its detail
from small beginnings,
colour it with bold brush strokes.
Engrave it on my heart in times of doubt.
Strengthen its design against
the winds of impossibility.
Give me arms outstretched
to catch the dreams of others,
help us to sketch hope in
the aftermath of pain.
Stand together in the shadows
of disappointment,
share in celebration as
dreams become reality.
Creator God, set a dream in my heart …
A dream of hope, a dream that will change
a moment, a day, a life:
For eternity.

WRITTEN FOR THE CARE FOR THE FAMILY
CHRISTMAS APPEAL LETTER, 2001.

A prayer for purpose …

What is your purpose for me, Lord?
To enjoy You – I know.
To worship You – as I am able.
To be Your hands and feet for Your people.

But what do You want me to DO, Lord?
How should I spend my days?

Hear the urgency in my desire, Lord God.
Feel the longing I have to serve You.

For I know that there is nothing greater I can do on earth.
No empires I can build.
No awards I can win.
No promotion I can secure,
That will give me more joy than to hear You say:

'Well done, good and faithful servant.'

Lord – show me Your purposes.

... And joy in finding purpose!

I worship You, wonderful God
That You have given me – ME! – this privilege:
To serve You with delight.
To do Your work with joy.
YIPPEE!
I can hardly believe that You have entrusted me with this.
But You have.
You prepared me, trained me, shaped
me for it – even before I knew.
You have handed over a part of Your work;
delegated the detail;
trusted me with the talent;
told me where to find the tools;
mentored me in my task.

And now You stand back in delight to watch me go!

Oh, Father!
Make me a faithful steward.
... And help me not to trip over my
own feet in my enthusiasm!

A prayer for Harvest Thanksgiving – according to Isaiah 58

Lord,
sometimes we think that Harvest Thanksgiving
should be like a trolley dash:
no spending and all satisfaction!
An over-the-top reminder of all You give
us pressed into two minutes.
A recognition of the abundance of Your love:
the overflowing basket of grace;
tottering heaps of goodness;
a pile of provision made up of so many shapes and sizes,
brands and boxes of life that we feel overwhelmed.
And it should.

But as we race to the checkout, remind us
that while all these goods are free,
out of them we must give as much as we
have received and more: three for two;
two for one; buy one, give one free.
Give and give and never give up giving.
For you require a very different kind
of spending and satisfaction ...

*'... spend yourselves on behalf of the hungry and
satisfy the needs of the oppressed ...' (Isaiah 58:10).*

Help us spend and satisfy according to Your ways Lord.

Amen.

Christmas

The wonder is not so much in the twinkle of the lights
as in the mysteries of the dark.
Not so much in the sound of bells and carols sung
as in the familiar cry of a newborn baby.
The joy is not so much in the yelps of satisfied getting
as in the silence of heaven's unfathomable giving.
Not so much in the deserved reward
but in the undeserved sacrifice.

As we unwrap this day, Lord God,
show us the One who gave us the ultimate gift.

Easter

From the deathly dark of Good Friday
to the life-giving light of Sunday;
from the hopeless silence of Saturday to
the 'rest of our lives' on Monday:
fill us with the knowledge of the wonder
and hope of You.

Amen.

Today

Today was a great day.
Today ticked the box … and packed it.
It tied the ribbon and put my name
on the label
next to Yours.
So here it is, Lord.
I give it back as a gift to You.

… And thank You!

Finding the heart of worship ...

'Yet a time is coming and has now come when the true worshippers will worship the Father in spirit and truth, for they are the kind of worshippers the Father seeks.'

John 4:23

Melt this heart for worship, Lord,
Make it burn within me.

Help me fill my mind with all that should be thought.
Help me find the words that say all that can be said.
Let my silences utter mysteries.
And my loud hallelujahs reach the halls of heaven.

Give me ways to worship
Days to worship
Nights to wonder.

For I long to worship You, Lord God,
In spirit and in truth.
Holy Spirit – help me find my heart of worship!

Words of worship

Staggering
Marvellous
Breathtaking
Awesome God
We worship You.

Almighty
Merciful
Just
and powerful God
We worship You.

Unchanging
Longsuffering
Constant
Faithful God
We worship You.

Wind-blowing
Rock-shaping
Energising
and ever-present God
We worship You.

Tender
Tantalising
Intimate
Beckoning God
We worship You.

Fathering
Forgiving
Welcoming
and homecoming God
We worship You.

Thanksgiving psalm

On your feet now – applaud GOD!
 Bring a gift of laughter,
  sing yourselves into his presence.

Know this: GOD is God, and God, GOD.
 He made us; we didn't make him.
  We're his people, his well-tended sheep.

Enter with the password: 'Thank you!'
 Make yourselves at home, talking praise.
  Thank him. Worship him.

For GOD is sheer beauty,
 all-generous in love,
  loyal always and ever.

PSALM 100:1–5, *THE MESSAGE*

The hope of heaven

Overwhelming welcome
Unimaginable peace
Inconceivable joy
Loving community
Boundless celebration
Perfect peace
Unknown intimacy
Eternal security …

HEAVEN!

Doxology

To him who is able to keep you from falling and to present you before his glorious presence without fault and with great joy – to the only God our Saviour be glory, majesty, power and authority, through Jesus Christ our Lord, before all ages, now and for evermore! Amen.

JUDE 24–25

And finally ...

Amen. Come, Lord Jesus.
The grace of the Lord Jesus be
with God's people. Amen.

REVELATION 22:20–21